Rebuild your Financial Ship
And set sail into a new Dimension
Of hope and prosperity

CONTENTS

Money Lessons,1,2,3,4,5..2

What is Bankruptcy?..11

Obtaining Your Credit Report 14

How to Use Your 3 Credit Reports..14

Why Check Your Report? 15

Credit Reports..15

Free Credit Reports..16

If your request for a free credit report is denied: 16

Credit Score 17

Credit Reporting Agencies 17

File a Complaint 18

Negative Information in a Credit Report 19

Fixing Errors in a Credit Report 19

File a complaint 20

Correcting Errors 20

Step One 20

Step Two 22

Make sure you are eligible 26

Submit your offer 26

If your offer is accepted 27

Get Help 28

How do we maintain financial balance? 29

Financial Blessings 34

Winning messages 35

MONEY LESSONS TO FINANCIAL BLESSINGS

This is a package of information and facts about how to change direction with difficult money matters, also some life stories of success and failure.

1. History of Money
2. Money Lessons: 1, 2, 3, 4
3. Budget Tools
4. FIX Mode, information on bankruptcy options, credit repair, and free credit reports, free tax help and tax resolution info.
5. How do we maintain financial balance?
6. Financial Blessings
7. Winning Messages

Here are examples of some affirmations to help encourage you in your process of financial recovery.

Curb your spending like you curb your appetite to lose pounds. Only then will you lose the weight of debt. The idea is to lift the heavy burden of debt, to feel lighter and increase your mobility to move more freely towards financial success.

Some industries survive on people never getting out of credit bondage. But, you can unlock yourself with the key of starting a simple budget process that has worked for countless others.

This is a low-cost report whose informational value far outweighs the price you pay.

James F. Lucas Jr

Tax Specialist and Notary public

The History of Money: concerns the development of means of carrying out transactions involving a medium of exchange. **Money** is any clearly identifiable object of value that is generally accepted as payment for goods and services and repayment of debts within a market or which is legal tender within a country.

Historically, we went from exchanging livestock, like chicken and cattle, to coins to paper money to plastic to now electronic transfers of money. The way we use money must be paid attention to because the idea for which we know how it's used can slip away with time. As we get older, we may find ourselves stuffing money under the mattress, thinking it's safe because of fear of a financial institution that is unknown.

Money Lesson 1: Money lessons are good teachers if we can learn and apply what was learned. These lessons are my stories, but you can tell yourself your own story. The first experience with money came when I was 4 or 5 years old. This lesson is about my first awareness of the value of money. I'm from New Haven Connecticut so there was always a store at the corner. My mother had just started to work and on her payday, she would give me and several kids at the babysitter's 5 cents. So, the bigger kids would take me to the store and we would buy lots of candy and I remembered that good feeling. Then after some time, my mother gave us all a nickel again, but this time she gave me a quarter. I didn't know what I had until I got to the store and was able to get more with my big nickel. Everyone I was with treated me special, the feeling was something to remember. The next time my mother gave out nickels I told her I wanted the one with the bird on it, I felt like I wanted to stay at that level of gratification. That was my first experience with money that gave me the message that if I had more than others they may treat me differently. Also, I see now that all through my life I saw more money, more power, but my truth now is more power is more love I receive and able to give.

Money Lesson 2: At this time in my life, I was about 5 or 6 years old and I was again near a corner store and they always sold lots of penny candy. I was able to freely come in and out of the house and play outside as long as I didn't go to the other corner, which was too busy and had some bad elements there. One day, I decided to try and capture that feeling again of having some money and going to the store with friends to buy that good old candy. I ran in the house and my mother was not around, so I skipped the process of asking her for some money and doing a dance if she didn't give it to me, and went straight to her pocketbook and took out a bill. I ran out of the house and to the corner store to show the kids what I had. I took them all in to buy them candy. Man, we had bags of candy and we were all very happy. I went home, and my mother confronted me about her money that was missing. I slowly started to understand that it was 5 dollars and I stole it from her, which was very bad as she started to wear my rear end out with a belt. I never took any money from my mother again. I learned a lesson not to steal from my mother and wish I could have applied that lesson to not take from myself, also needed to practice that with others as well. Give and be given or take and it will be taken from you in one way or another.

What I understood from that experience is that money is so important to people that they will hurt you over it, physically, like the discipline I got or emotional pain, like people not wanting to be close to you anymore unless you give them the money they asked you for. Also, mental pain when people will say things to you that aren't true, only to manipulate you to get and have your money. So, the exchange of money with anyone must have some precaution with it, because there can be some real pain in the end. Some friendships that are lost because of money may not be worth the friendship if it means always getting hurt over money and if they leave you they were not your friend to begin with. Do we want love or hate in the exchange of money? Having the right attitude before and after helps me survive any loss of money or people. I later found out that if you can't give money to a friend that asks for money and they don't want to be your friend because of that, well they probably weren't your friend to begin with.

Money Lesson 3: Most of my young life I associated love with money, so I thought. My mother gave me money and it made me feel happy. When she didn't give it to me it made me feel sad. I did have the self- centeredness of a child and most people grow out of this, but I didn't right away. I grew up with the idea that every time my mother gave me something, especially money, that it was love. So, I got confused early on in life misplacing my values. Understanding now that love is expressed in many more ways than giving money and material things. Love most importantly now that I see, comes in the form of advice, lessons, hugs, listening, and discipline etc. When I was about 12 years old my mother decided to change things. She started giving me an allowance each week of $10 on Friday. I embraced this idea because it was a big amount of money to me in 1969. So, now my mother is about budgeting her money and she is having some expectation that I am going to do the same. I later found out there was not a lot of room for error. This first opportunity to budget my money that my mother gave me I failed at, if it meant I had to hold onto some of it during the week. Once I got my allowance on Friday I never had any money by Sunday. It was like pulling teeth to get another dime from my mother because it meant her having to readjust her budget that she was trying to stick to. I felt like I was trying to recapture that same feeling I had when I got the nickel with the bird on it. So, if I did the same thing my mother was doing with her money we both would have been on the same page, but instead, I spent my money as soon as I could, like there was no tomorrow and tomorrow always came and I always found myself broke. My mother practiced some principles and I didn't have a clue. I had a friend that lived down the street from me that showed me $10 in his wallet one day and showed me the same $10 a week later. I remember saying to myself "Wow that's crazy, holding onto his money, What's that all about.? He later became a banker and maintains his finances well. When I got to be 19 years old my mother once again tried to teach me something about money, but this time it was through tough love. At this time in my life, I had no job and I was still asking my mother for money. My mother said to me at this time that she was cutting me off from giving me any money and I was shocked. She tried to help me understand about her enabling me, which she discovered was wrong, but I thought at first that she was the meanest mother in the world. She then explained.

I will be ok, just go out and get a job and hold onto your money. She said that when a person needs to eat or have shelter, self-preservation takes place and like animals, we look to survive. I knew my mother was serious because like a child I tested her, and she never gave in, not even for .50 cents. So, I was almost forced to get my own money and try to hold onto it and today I'm grateful for the lessons my mother and others tried to give me. I say others because some of the ideas my mother gave me, I'm sure came from her therapist. My mother passed away 4 years later.

Money Lessons 4: I took some of my mixed ideas I learned on the road of life with me practicing some, and failing to practice others, which caused me to have a great deal of imbalance in my life and in my finances. In my adult life, I always tried to manage my finances by moving things around, like refinancing getting another credit card to pay off another. I kept some ways and means to survive but never concentrated on a budget. What did help from time to time that got me out of the dark to see where I was and where I was going was a budget on the spot. It was like a spot inventory to get the bigger picture for the moment. As I lived on in my adult life I noticed a progression in my poor money management. I made and got lots of money but couldn't hold onto it, no matter how much I was getting. I always went to my dark place of not seeing the full reality of my finances. It was like the debt grew in the dark and died in the light of exposure. By the time I got to my 30s I had mortgaged the house up to $100,000 from $5,000. I also picked up some habits that gave me some personal problems which were expensive and all mind and mood-altering stuff, chemical and non-chemical, all putting me further into darkness. When I turned 36 I had reached a bottom by using all these external things to fill the void I didn't know I had and losing almost everything. I lost the house, the good job, the car and almost my family. In 1994 I was given the gift of desperation because I became willing to do whatever was necessary to change and even the things I didn't want to do like budgeting or seeking help from others, which is very humbling. The hardest thing I had to change was what was at the core of my being because nothing else would last if I did nothing to change. I first focused on changing myself at the core and everything else started to fall into place. I began to maintain myself and my spirituality, which kept me out of that dark place I once knew. I started to get my finances back in order and, at the same time, I knew I had to keep the inner spirit lit so I could keep my sight of where I've been, where I am and where I want to go. I began to take a weekly budget, to take my financial inventory and, at the same time, take my own inventory, simultaneously. Since my surrender in 1994, I have not gone back to that dark place. I have had two homes, put my kids through college and saved some money; then I retired from my government job at age 55. The skill that I developed in college, taking accounting in 1976, has come to life in 1996, in the form of tax preparation and I still love to do taxes today. All is well with my new way to live but not without the foundation of budgeting and principles. Timothy 6:10 says that" it is the love of money that is the root of all evil" and I also say it's the love of spending which adds to the problem. The SALE can always be a trigger to get off track and blow the budget up. My lesson is changed at the core and with money, I save some, give some, but not grudgingly, and spend some, but not without a BUDGET.

Money Lesson 5: Scheming on myself. In the late 70s I had this mentality that the only way to get ahead in life is to have some kind of scheme to help you rise to the top. They called it getting over or you got blessed. Today they call this scheming dishonesty, doing the wrong thing to get something you want. In the late 70s I met a young man in college from New York who I got to know. When I was in college I had little to no money. As I got to know my New York friend I noticed he wasn't as broke as I was. He wore nicer clothes, had a new car and a nice furnished apartment. Over time I started to get to my New York friend enough to ask questions. I became curious as to how he was paying for this life style without a visible job. When got to know him better, he started to tell me what he was doing and how it works. He took me under his wing and treated me like his younger brother. He showed me what he was doing financially. He told me he had a business that ran from his apartment. He said he was manipulating credit cards to get lots of capital to invest in business. Doing this by using the business he had to apply for credit and give his self, income and employment verification. I noticed at this time my friend had no other business except the business phone at his apartment. He later showed me some evidence beyond what he was doing, by taking me to New York. I met some of his friends who was further along in this idea. They had a store on Lenox avenue, with merchandise they bought with manipulated credit. The store owners had the appearance of doing well, they had nice clothes, new cars, and other nice things. They had the look of success and the glory of this idea or scheme. So, I was inspired to try this at my home. I purchased a business phone. I started filling out applications for credit in my name and others. I later got credit and money through this process and it felt good. It felt so good with the money, that it got in the way of the second part of the plan. Which was to invest in a business, I got stuck like chuck. The result was I ruined my credit in the short term and nothing else happened. The end of the story for the others was they failed, and one went to jail. Please don't try this its wrong and it dose not work especially now a day. Also, if you are like me I value my conscious and I like to sleep at night. Bottom line is I schemed on myself, by cheating myself out of establishing credit the right way and hurting my idea of what real success is. Lesson is quick money is not always a great IDEA.

Budget Tools: I was always impressed with the stories my cousin in New Jersey told me about managing her money. Especially the one she told me about how she had some discipline to go to the bank every time she got paid to save some of her earnings. She would tell me it doesn't matter how much you save because it will eventually add up to something. I was in awe when she said she bought her last two brand new cars with cash. My first thought was I will never be able to do that; that was in 1982. Now, I believe I can and will. Today my reliance is not totally on credit security only, it's on keeping balance in my totality of credit, cash savings, and spiritual core being. If you want to change from not budgeting to budgeting it will bring on the great source of fear. That's why getting courage from somewhere is a necessary part of the change.

Budgeting regularly is like setting up an intervention for yourself, in case we get off course. We will have to stop and think of the finances in place to catch us when we want to act out or just slide off the path unintentionally.

Life events can occur unexpectedly and knock us off our square financially. For example, accidental losses of cars, homes, jobs, health issues, etc. If we even have a small practice of budgeting, we can use that to reset our foundation and rebuild what was lost and sometimes more depending on how much our core spiritual being has been reset with a stronger drive to come back. A good attitude can help us take off, like saying I am down but not out with no place to go but up.

I will mention a setback I once had while doing well with a good budget in place but, when my kids went to college I had some unexpected expenses that arose besides the tuition, like computers, cars, special housing and spending money to keep them focused. My credit card debt rose to $30,000 at that time. Having good things in place helped rescue a budget soldier like me. I had available credit like I still have today at the lowest rate; I had savings and a cash flow. Also, I had a side business that provided a seasonal income from doing taxes. I worked overtime at my job just enough to provide pocket money for my kids while they went to college, but not now. After my kids graduated from college, I kept budgeting my way back to sound financial health. Along with my balance with faith that kept me healthy at my spiritual core, which is equally as important if not more, things snapped back. I lost a home, bought one and paid it off and then bought a new home. When my kids graduated from college, got jobs and left home in a short period of time I was able to make some conservative changes. I stayed away from buying things that I dreamed of right away like a Mercedes car or a new home. The extra money that I didn't have to use for my kids I put more money into my employer 401K and it was one of the best decisions I could make. I'm still retired at 59 and my wife retired from her job last year and we live in a newly built home. The home may not be our dream home, but we now have 3 bathrooms instead of our old one.

Budgeting can also be looked at as putting and keeping your finger on your own pulse. Just like we take our blood pressure to see if we need to change our medication or get a healthier diet, so do we with budgeting. We do a budget to see what needs to be changed, with spending or getting more income. In my experience with life and as it relates to finance, things always change. Since I started to depend on a budget in my life instead of some instincts I have, I have been able to stay with my reality and move with the cloud so to speak. Budgeting has helped me roll with the ups and downs of life. Over time I now realize that if I fall financially, I do have the faith that I can get back up with my budget skills. If I have no money to budget, I know I have one other thing to budget and that is my spirit. So as long as I keep my spirit lit, I can have fire or desire for getting money at some point to restart my life again.

I have put together for you a sample budget sheet that you can copy and practice on.

INCOME		EXPENSES	
CASH	_____	Mtg/Rent	_____
		ELECTRIC	_____
SALARIES	_____	GAS	_____
		PHONES	_____
		CABLE	_____
		INTERNET	_____
		MEDICAL	_____
		CAR INS	_____
		LIFE INS	_____
		2ND MTG	_____
		CAR LOAN	_____
		CHILDCARE	_____
		CAR GAS	_____
		VISA	_____
		MASTER	_____
		CREDIT	_____
		PET CARE	_____
		ALLOWANCE	_____
		SAVINGS	_____
		MISC.	_____
		MISC.	_____
		MISC.	_____

TOTAL INCOME _____ >CARRY FOWARD> >_____

TOTAL EXPENSES _____

BALANCE POSITIVE SAVED BALANCE NEGATIVE CUT BACK EXP._____ > C/F

FIX MODE: Get into your fix mode, which is being solution driven, but first, make sure you have gotten some practice with budgeting first. Budgeting can and will assist with changing the process but equally as important is some change in our core spiritual being. It may only be a quick fix if we just rearrange a few things. Some of our shame and guilt at our core left unaddressed can paralyze us, preventing us from moving forward in our lives. Some of our most meaningful amends can be acting differently in the present. We may feel bad at the core and not know it's from wasting our money and not being responsible in taking care of ourselves and our family. Long lasting change happens when we discover and recover our core spiritual being. One of my examples is when I got on my path of change I discovered that family is important to me so as I looked deeper into my life I became more aware of my need to find any of my father's family who I didn't know for myself and my kids. I was about 44 years old and I looked up my father's fathers family first and I did this before all the internet searches we have today. I was able to gather some documents and make some phone calls and write some letters, which in the end resulted in a phone call to my father's half-sister, which open the door to other family. As I continued in my fix mode I found my half-sister, which I always knew of her but didn't have the willingness or help to find her, but when I did we connected. My sister and I then formed a relationship over the years and we still talk and that was a blessing or a benefit of fix mode.

I think the same principle applies to changing our financial problems at the core. By resolving any tax debt, we must get the help we need and then stick to the plan in order to have a long-lasting change take place; otherwise, it will only become a quick fix.

Having a budget in place or being able to do one on the spot is helpful when using one of these help sources of the offer in compromise, credit repair, credit counseling, or any of the bankruptcy options. Because being familiar with a budget means we are familiar with our financial picture, which means we can communicate to any help source quickly what we need help with.

There is more to what meets the eye. In a fixed mode, this saying means when you look at your finances at first glance there is more of the unseen problems in attitudes ideas and behaviors that may go undetected if we don't look longer and deeper into our money matters.

The next few pages include an offer in compromise and tax resolution information and contact information. Bankruptcy option information, free credit report and error correction info and contact information, free tax help and where to go for it and 401K savings tips. If you can't do any of these things on your own, please see free help sources first. This step of finding free sources can also help you get traction as you get started in your fix mode.

What is Bankruptcy?

Bankruptcy allows individuals, couples, and businesses that cannot meet their financial obligations to be excused from repaying some or all their debt. Bankruptcy has been in existence since ancient times. In the United States, the rules and procedures for filing bankruptcy are governed by federal law. States are prohibited from legislating in this area of the law.

There are two types of bankruptcy. In a liquidation bankruptcy, debtors must surrender their property, which is sold, and the proceeds distributed to creditors. In return, all debts are permanently discharged. In a reorganization bankruptcy, debtors are allowed to keep their property. But the debtors must agree to an installment plan to repay creditors a portion of the amount they owe.

Filing for bankruptcy involves submitting a petition and fee to the bankruptcy court. The fee is close to $300 for most personal bankruptcies. The petition will contain sworn statements by the debtors concerning the amount of money they owe, their income and expenses, as well as a complete list of all their assets. After filing, a court hearing is held to review the information in the petition.

Chapter 7 bankruptcies are by far the most common. These are liquidation bankruptcies in which the debtors must turn over all "non-exempt" property to a supervising officer known as the bankruptcy trustee. Property is exempt if it falls within specific categories of assets that debtors are allowed to keep their property, such as a certain amount of clothing, household items, tools for work, and in some instances, vehicles and the family home.

The Chapter 7 trustee will take the debtor's non-exempt property (if there is any), and sell it. The money will be paid to the debtor's creditors. This may result in creditors receiving a small fraction of their claims. The balance of the debtor's loans and obligations are forgiven and can never be collected. Creditors who attempt to collect debts that have been discharged face severe penalties under federal law.

The fact that a liquidation bankruptcy wipes out debt completely is obviously attractive to anyone who cannot afford to pay their bills. But what about people who have non-exempt property that they do not want to give up? Chapter 13 is a reorganization bankruptcy. It allows debtors to keep their property by agreeing to make monthly payments toward their debt over the course of three to five years.

Chapter 13 bankruptcies offer many benefits besides allowing debtors to keep their property. For example, certain types of secured debt, like a car loan, can be restructured by reducing principal to the market value of the collateral and lowering payments by extending the repayment period to 60 months. Other obligations, like mortgages, student loans, and tax liabilities can be modified as well. Creditors are given no choice in the matter.

Bankruptcy is not available to everyone. Those who have had their debts discharged in Chapter 7 within the past eight years cannot re-file. For Chapter 13, the waiting period is six years. Too much disposable income is also a problem. Congress has established a "means test" for this purpose. Debtors who make enough money to repay their creditors will be barred from filing a liquidation bankruptcy, through reorganization may be an option.

Businesses that have become insolvent but want to stay in business may be able to file a Chapter 11 bankruptcy. Like a personal reorganization, Chapter 11 allows businesses to obtain protection from their creditors while they put together a repayment plan. Liabilities can be reduced and restructured to give the business another chance at achieving profitability.

Whether a debtor is considering filing under Chapter 7, 11, or 13, they must comply with a vast number of federal laws and regulations. An error at any step of the process can result in the court refusing to discharge the debtor's liabilities. When the bankruptcy process ends this way, the consequences are disastrous. With so much at stake, hiring a licensed bankruptcy attorney at the outset is a wise investment.

Seek an attorney that offers an initial free consultation before making any decisions.

Credit repair: The important thing here is you can start this yourself and if you need help you, can seek out a credit counseling agency, but make sure they are not going to charge you a lot of upfront fees and make a lot of unrealistic promises. Start your credit repair with getting your free credit report, and contact information here.

3 Free Credit Reports per Year: How to Get Free Copies

The three free credit reports consumers may request per year provide important information and a means to help consumers protect against identity fraud. The information contained is invaluable. As a consumer, you may request a free copy of your credit report from each of the three national credit bureaus every twelve months. Accessing and reviewing your credit reports from each of the three bureaus annually helps you ensure the accuracy of the information. It also allows you to monitor your account history to protect against identity theft.

Obtaining Your Credit Report

To find out how to get your annual credit report from each bureau, visit AnnualCreditReport.com. This site helps consumers obtain their free credit reports as required by the Fair and Accurate Credit Transactions Act (FACT Act). To request for your free credit reports online at the site, you will need to provide specific information, including your name, social security number, and address. You will then be asked to select which of the credit bureaus you want to obtain your report from:

- TransUnion
- Experian
- Equifax

You will also be required to answer a set of questions to verify your identity. The information contained in these questions comes directly from your credit reports.

You can obtain a credit report from each of these agencies without charge one time per 12-month period. To create ongoing protection for yourself, consider obtaining one report every four months. This ensures you can consistently monitor your accounts.

How to Use Your 3 Credit Reports

Once you obtain a copy of your reports, you'll be able to see what potential creditors and other permitted parties see about your credit history. This information will help potential creditors decide if they should lend to you. The reports contain the following types of information:

• Your name and address

• Your current open accounts, including balances, payment history, and highest balance

• Your closed accounts, unless they are over seven years old

• Records of inquiries by all parties that obtained a credit report on you from that credit bureau

• Public records occurring in the last 10 years

You can also follow the instructions provided on the site to report any inaccuracies in your report. You will not receive a copy of your credit score with your free annual credit reports. To request your credit score, you need to visit the website of one of the three credit bureaus and generally pay a fee to do so.

Why Check Your Report?

By checking your credit reports regularly, you may verify their accuracy. If you find inaccuracies, you should report them to the appropriate credit bureau so that they will not impact your credit profile. Additionally, knowing what is on your credit reports may help you make proper credit decisions about your future.

Credit Reports

Credit reports contain information about your bill payment history, loans, current debt, and other financial information. They show where you work and live and whether you've been sued, arrested, or filed for bankruptcy.

Credit reports help lenders decide whether to extend you credit or approve a loan and determine what interest rate they will charge you. Prospective employers, insurers, and rental property owners may also look at your credit report.

It's important to check your credit report regularly to ensure that your personal information and financial accounts are being accurately reported and that no fraudulent accounts have been opened in your name. If you find errors on your credit report, take steps to have them corrected.

Free Credit Reports

You are entitled to a free credit report from each of the three credit reporting agencies (Equifax, Experian, and TransUnion) once every 12 months. You can request all three reports at once, or space them out throughout the year. Learn about other situations in which you can request a free credit report.

Request your free credit report:

Online: Visit AnnualCreditReport.com

By Phone: Call 1-877-322-8228. Deaf and hard of hearing consumers can access the TTY service by calling 711 and referring the Relay Operator to 1-800-821-7232.

By Mail: Complete the Annual Credit Report Request Form (PDF, Download Adobe Reader) and mail it to:

Annual Credit Report Request Service

PO Box 105281

Atlanta, GA 30348-5281

If your request for a free credit report is denied:

Contact the credit reporting agency (CRA) directly to try and resolve the issue. The CRA should inform you of the reason they denied your request and explain what to do next. Often, you will only need to provide information that was missing or incorrect on your application for a free credit report.

If you are unable to resolve your dispute with the CRA, contact the Consumer Financial Protection Bureau (CFPB).

Credit Score

A credit score is a number that rates your credit risk at one point in time. It can help creditors determine whether to give you credit, decide the terms you are offered or the rate you will pay for the loan. Having a high score can benefit you in many ways, including making it easier for you to obtain a loan, rent an apartment, and lower your insurance rate.

The information in your credit report is used to calculate your credit score. A credit score as calculated based on your:

- payment history
- balances outstanding
- length of your credit history
- applications for new credit accounts
- types of credit accounts (mortgages, car loans, credit cards)

It's important to make sure your credit report is accurate because it can affect the accuracy of a credit score. You can have multiple credit scores, created by different companies or lenders that use their own credit scoring system.

Your free annual credit report does not include your credit score, but it's available, often for a fee. You can get your credit score, from several sources, such as your credit card statement or buying it from one of the three major credit reporting agencies. When you buy your score, you often get information on how you can improve it.

Credit Reporting Agencies

A credit reporting agency (CRA) is a company that collects information about where you live, and work, how you pay your bills, whether you have been sued, arrested, or filed for bankruptcy. All this information is combined in a credit report. A CRA will then sell your credit report to creditors, employers, insurers, and others. These companies will use these reports to make decisions about extending credit, jobs, and insurance policies to you.

You are entitled to order (every 12 months) a free copy of your credit report from each of the major credit reporting agencies (Equifax, Experian, and TransUnion) through AnnualCreditReport.com. This website is the only one that is government authorized to provide you with free copies of your credit report.

You can also contact the credit agencies directly if you need to dispute information in your report, place a fraud alert or security freeze on your credit file, or have other questions.

- Equifax or by phone at 1-866-349-5191
- Experian or by phone at 1-888-397-3742
- TransUnion or by phone at 1-800-916-8800

File a Complaint

Credit reporting agencies are not operated by the government, but you can still file a complaint about them with the federal government. Some reasons for filing a complaint include:

- dissatisfaction with the outcome of a dispute with a CRA
- the CRA doesn't respond to your dispute request
- credit report was used improperly

- inability to get a copy of a credit report or score
- problems with credit monitoring or identity protection services.

File a complaint about a credit reporting agency to the Consumer Financial Protection Bureau online or by phone at 1-855-411-2372.

Errors on Your Credit Report

If you find errors on your credit report, write a letter disputing the errors and send it (along with supporting documentation) to the following:

- Credit reporting agency (Equifax, Experian, or TransUnion)
- Information provider (bank, credit card company, or other organization that provided the credit reporting agency with inaccurate information)

Find a sample dispute letter and get detailed instructions on how to report errors.

Under the Fair Credit Reporting Act, both the credit reporting agency (CRA) and the information provider are responsible for correcting inaccurate or incomplete information in your credit report.

If the errors have not been corrected after you've disputed them in writing, you can file a complaint with the Consumer Financial Protection Bureau (CFPB).

Negative Information in a Credit Report

Negative information in a credit report can include public records-- tax liens, judgments, bankruptcies--that provide insight into your financial status and obligations. A credit reporting company generally can report most negative information for seven years.

Information about a lawsuit or a judgment against you can be reported for seven years or until the statute of limitations runs out, whichever is longer. Bankruptcies can be kept on your report for up to 10 years, and unpaid tax liens for 15 years.

Fixing Errors in a Credit Report

Anyone who denies you credit, housing, insurance, or a job because of a credit report must give you the name, address, and telephone number of the credit reporting agency (CRA) that provided the report. Under the Fair Credit Reporting Act (FCRA), you have the right to request a free report within 60 days if a company denies you credit based on the report.

You can get your credit report fixed if it contains inaccurate or incomplete information:

- Contact both the credit reporting agency and the company that provided the information to the CRA.

- Tell the CRA, in writing, what information you believe is inaccurate. Keep a copy of all correspondence.

Some companies may promise to repair or fix your credit for an upfront fee--but there is no way to remove negative information in your credit report if it is accurate.

File a complaint

If you have a problem with credit reporting, you can file a complaint with the Consumer

Financial Protection Bureau (CFPB).

ALSO, there are ways to apply solutions through the credit reporting agencies.

Correcting Errors

Under the FCRA, both the credit reporting company and the

information provider (that is, the person, company, or organization that provides information about you to a credit reporting company) are responsible for correcting inaccurate or incomplete information in your report. To take advantage of all your rights under this law, contact the credit reporting company and the information provider.

Step One

Tell the credit reporting company, in writing, what information you think is inaccurate. Use our sample dispute letter. Include copies (NOT originals) of documents that support your position. In addition to providing your complete name and address, your letter should clearly identify each item in your report you dispute, state the facts and explain why you dispute the information and request that it be removed or corrected. You may want to enclose a copy of your report with the items in question circled. Send your letter by certified mail, "return receipt requested," so you can document what the credit reporting company received. Keep copies of your dispute letter and enclosures.

Credit reporting companies must investigate the items in question — usually within 30 days — unless they consider your dispute frivolous. They also must forward all the relevant data you provide about the inaccuracy to the organization that provided the information. After the information provider receives notice of a dispute from the credit reporting company, it must investigate, review the relevant information, and report the results back to the credit reporting company. If the information provider finds the disputed information is inaccurate, it must notify all three nationwide credit reporting companies, so they can correct the information in your file.

When the investigation is complete, the credit reporting company must give you the results in writing and a free copy of your report if the dispute results in a change. This free report does not count as your annual free report. If an item is changed or deleted, the credit reporting company cannot put the disputed information back in your file unless the information provider verifies that it is accurate and complete. The credit reporting company also must send you written notice that includes the name, address, and phone number of the information provider.

If you ask, the credit reporting company must send notices of any corrections to anyone who received your report in the past six months. You can have a corrected copy of your report sent to anyone who received a copy during the past two years for employment purposes.

If an investigation doesn't resolve your dispute with the credit reporting company, you can ask that a statement of the dispute be included in your file and in future reports. You also can ask the credit reporting company to provide your statement to anyone who received a copy of your report in the recent past. You can expect to pay a fee for this service.

Step Two

Tell the information provider (that is, the person, company, or organization that provides information about you to a credit reporting company), in writing, that you dispute an item in your credit report. Use this sample dispute letter. Include copies (NOT originals) of documents that support your position. If the provider listed an address on your credit report, send your letter to that address. If no address is listed, contact the provider and ask for the correct address to send your letter. If the information provider does not give you an address, you can send your letter to any business address for that provider.

If the provider continues to report the item you disputed to a credit reporting company, it must let the credit reporting company know about your dispute. And if you are correct — that is, if the information you dispute is found to be inaccurate or incomplete — the information provider must tell the credit reporting company to update or delete the item.

About Your File

Your credit file may not reflect all your credit accounts. Although most national department store and all-purpose bank credit card accounts will be included in your file, not all creditors supply information to credit reporting companies: some local retailers, credit unions, travel, entertainment, and gasoline card companies are among the creditors that don't.

When negative information in your report is accurate, only the passage of time can assure its removal. A credit reporting company can report most accurate negative information for seven years and bankruptcy information for 10 years. Information about an unpaid judgment against you can be reported for seven years or until the statute of limitations runs out, whichever is longer. There is no time limit on reporting: information about criminal convictions; information reported in response to your application for a job that pays more than $75,000 a year; and information reported because you've applied for more than $150,000 worth of credit or life insurance. There is a standard method for calculating the seven-year reporting period. Generally, the period runs from the date that the event took place.

Use this sample to draft a letter disputing errors on your credit report.

Your letter should clearly identify each item in your report you dispute, state the facts and explain why you dispute the information and request that it be removed or corrected. You may want to enclose a copy of your report with the items in question circled.

Send your letter by certified mail, "return receipt requested," so you can document what the credit reporting company received. Remember to include copies of the applicable enclosures and save copies for your files.

[Your Name]

[Your Address]

[Your City, State, Zip Code]

[Date]

Complaint Department,

[Company Name]

[Street Address]

[City, State, Zip Code]

Dear Sir or Madam:

I am writing to dispute the following information in my file. I have circled the items I dispute on the attached copy of the report I received.

This item **[identify the item(s) disputed by name of source, such as creditors or tax court, and identify the type of item, such as credit account, judgment, etc.]** is **[inaccurate or incomplete]** because **[describe what is inaccurate or incomplete and why]**. I am requesting that the item be removed **[or request another specific change]** to correct the information.

Enclosed are copies of **[use this sentence if applicable and describe any enclosed documentation, such as payment records and court documents]** supporting my position. Please reinvestigate this **[these]** matter**[s]** and **[delete or correct]** the disputed item**[s]** as soon as possible.

Sincerely,

Your name

Enclosures: **[List what you are enclosing.]**

Tips, sometimes it's a good idea to contact the attorney related to the debt owed before you pay anything or set up a new payment plan because it's possible you may be able to negotiate a low payoff figure or one without interest.

How Long Can Old Debts Be Collected?

Each state has a law referred to as a "statute of limitations," which spells out the time during which creditors or collectors may sue borrowers to collect debts. In most states, they run between 4-6 years after the last payment was made on the debt.

Please be advised, if you're able to get the company to charge off any debt sometimes this is called a debt cancelation which can be considered income on a 1099-C. check with your tax advisor to help prepare you for any unexpected taxes on this income.

Fix mode: Tax debt remedies help and it's important to know which ones best fit your financial picture. It's important to know that if you owe back taxes this is called a federal debt, which can be very burdensome. The IRS is one of the most powerful government agencies in the entire government if they get a levy when collecting they can garnish your wages and put a lien on your property, also freeze and take your money from your bank accounts. One thing that many don't know until it's little too late is when you apply for a mortgage most mortgage companies will not give you a mortgage unless you pay off all your back taxes or in rare situations have a solid payment plan. That's why it's not good to owe the IRS and they're very strict in charging interest and penalties until you pay them off or freeze the process while negotiating an offer in compromise or another option is to contact the tax advocacy group which is free and very helpful. Here is some information to sink your teeth into.

An offer in compromise allows you to settle your tax debt for less than the full amount you owe. It may be a legitimate option if you can't pay your full tax liability, or doing so creates a financial hardship. We consider your unique set of facts and circumstances:

- Ability to pay;
- Income;
- Expenses; and
- Asset equity.

We generally approve an offer in compromise when the amount offered represents the most we can expect to collect within a reasonable period of time. Explore all other payment options before submitting an offer in compromise. The Offer in Compromise program is not for everyone. If you hire a tax professional to help you file an offer, be sure to check his or her qualifications.

Make sure you are eligible

Before we can consider your offer, you must be current with all filing and payment requirements. You are not eligible if you are in an open bankruptcy proceeding. Use the Offer in Compromise Pre-Qualifier to confirm your eligibility and prepare a preliminary proposal.

Submit your offer

You'll find step-by-step instructions and all the forms for submitting an offer in the Offer in Compromise Booklet, Form 656-B (PDF). Your completed offer package will include:

- Form 433-A (OIC) (individuals) or 433-B (OIC) (businesses) and all required documentation as specified on the forms;

- Form 656(s) - individual and business tax debt (Corporation/ LLC/ Partnership) must be submitted on separate Form 656;
- $186 application fee (non-refundable); and
- Initial payment (non-refundable) for each Form 656.

Select a payment option

Your initial payment will vary based on your offer and the payment option you choose:

- Lump Sum Cash: Submit an initial payment of 20 percent of the total offer amount with your application. If your offer is accepted, you will receive written confirmation. Any remaining balance due on the offer is paid in five or fewer payments.
- Periodic Payment: Submit your initial payment with your application. Continue to pay the remaining balance in monthly installments while the IRS considers your offer. If accepted, continue to pay monthly until it is paid in full.

If you meet the Low-Income Certification guidelines, you do not have to send the application fee or the initial payment and you will not need to make monthly installments during the evaluation of your offer. See your application package for details.

Understand the process.

While your offer is being evaluated:

- Your non-refundable payments and fees will be applied to the tax liability (you may designate payments to a specific tax year and tax debt);
- A Notice of Federal Tax Lien may be filed;
- Other collection activities are suspended;
- The legal assessment and collection period is extended;

- Make all required payments associated with your offer;
- You are not required to make payments on an existing installment agreement; and
- Your offer is automatically accepted if the IRS does not make a determination within two years of the IRS receipt date.

If your offer is accepted

- You must meet all the Offer Terms listed in Section 8 of Form 656, including filing all required tax returns and making all payments;
- Any refunds due within the calendar year in which your offer is accepted will be applied to your tax debt;
- Federal tax liens are not released until your offer terms are satisfied; and
- Certain offer information is available for public review at designated IRS offices.

If your offer is rejected

- You may appeal a rejection within 30 days using Request for Appeal of Offer in Compromise, Form 13711 (PDF).
- The online self-help tool may provide additional assistance on appealing your rejected offer.
- **Payments Topics**
- Understanding Your IRS Notice or Letter
- Foreign Electronic Payments
- Electronic Payment of User Fees
- Find all you need to consider and make an offer in Form 656-B, Offer in Compromise Booklet (PDF)

Get Help

- Offer in Compromise FAQs
- Video: Completing Form 656
- Understanding Your IRS Notice or Letter
- Owe Taxes? Understanding IRS Collection Efforts
- Download Forms

Pub. 594: IRS Collection Process

Explains the actions IRS may take to recover taxes owed. Download Pub. 594 (PDF)

Page Last Reviewed or Updated: 29-Sep-2017

Make sure you are familiar with your budget before applying for the offer in compromise. It's very much needed in understanding what you and they can see as to what you can pay and if you can pay. If you find that you can't fill out the application, then, seek help first from the tax person who did your taxes during the tax season. It's probably best to have this done with your tax person during the off-season when it's less busy.

 Free help from the tax advocacy service, contact 1877-777-4778 or taxpayeradvocate.irs.gov Free tax preparation help from VITA if your income is below 54k call 1800-906-9887 or irs.gov

How do we maintain financial balance?

Maintaining financial balance means having more than just a negative balance, it means having more money than a zero balance somewhere, like in the bank. Saving money is a way to help keep some financial balance and of course, having a lot of it can help us avoid the tilt in our household. Balancing at our core is still the foundation on which we build our financial wealth. Americans still don't save like they used to years ago, so why can't Americans save more money?

When personal-finance columnists explain America's poor saving habits, they sometimes start with the aspects of the human mind that make it challenging to plan. Behavioral psychology is a useful scapegoat for many foibles. But the decline in savings is recent, and the human brain hasn't evolved since the Ford administration. The bottom 90 % of households saved 10 % of their income in the first Reagan administration. By 2006, their savings rate was nearly negative-10 %.

There are a lot of theories like we stopped saving when our incomes stopped growing. The poor and middle class are in deeper debt and they are the biggest consumers that keep the economy afloat. They are always being pushed to the edge by super mass media to buy and spend your money, even if you don't have any they will always suggest for you to use your credit card as though that option is always supposed to be used. I feel your credit should never be used impulsively without a pause or a thought about if you can afford it, if you need it and you plan on buying it today.

Other theories are that the United States policies are not making it easier to save. It's not much incentive to save in the banks because there are fees and a very low return on your money. Years ago, we used to encourage saving even to kids with passbook savings accounts, which they have almost completely done away with. So, if we're not encouraged to save then we spend. Also, there is the pressure to keep up with the rich or as they say keeping up with the Jones or in other words people living above their means.

All of these pressures to help us fail at being a consumer and keeping financial balance leads me to believe that it's more important to keep the balance at your core spiritual being, to help fight back the pressures of the financial world that can cause us to tilt and then sink like the Titanic. So, like the Titanic ship, there was nothing that was going to stop it from sinking. If we're aware that we are on that ship financially speaking, and we move from room to room like going from credit card to credit card and not get off the ship to be rescued and reach the shore, which will give us our only hope to reset our finances and start over. Then, we may be in some sort of denial until we finally say abandon SHIP.

My own personal experience with a balance of my finances started in 1994 and hasn't ended yet. All because I believe it's due to my surrender to what wasn't working for me and I embraced a new way to live my life when I started to work my way back up or in other words rebuild my ship.

I had my wife give me two dollars per day to buy coffee in 1994 when I started to rebuild my ship, but only this time it wasn't called the Titanic. My ship could be called partner-ship because I partnered with many to rebuild my ship, so it can sail once again and how I help my ship continue to sail is with maintaining some principles in my life, like honesty, faith, willingness, discipline, and being consistent. After practicing some humility with my $2.00 per day budget and allowing my wife to be my partner in helping me manage my finances, I then moved up gradually towards taking more responsibility. I opened a savings account which was safe for me to put my money somewhere away from having cash and myself. I was still fresh out of bankruptcy from a few years ago, but I didn't lose hope. After getting and maintaining a savings account and getting a checking account, I applied for a high-interest rate credit card with a $500 balance and got it, to my surprise. I then valued that credit card and paid on time and never looked back from there. Later I was able to get a few more credit cards to rebuild my credit. I later got a car loan, which I paid on time and later paid off successfully. I was introduced to budgeting in the 90s that helped me keep balance and an eye on where I'm at and where I wanted to go. Kind of like my map theory, you have to see that you are here where the arrow states and then you can find the directions. I have consistently maintained very good credit since the 1990s and I developed some integrity.

Financially going from being on the Titanic ship to the partnership, partner-shipping with people, institutions, and principles, I had to pause in my writing to help my wife peel potatoes because it is important to do what is necessary to help maintain my partnership with my wife. Which means doing my part in the kitchen and around the house. Always keeping my side of the house or as they say my side of the street clean, including my finances that I'm in charge of. I try not to create problems with my credit use or deplete my savings. This will eventually put a burden on my wife and partnership. As I kept saving what I was able to comfortably save, over time or years I kept myself in position to take advantage of opportunities that came about, where I had more income. It gave me a choice of either spend more or save more. I most of the time chose to save, spend and give to myself and others in some type of way. This became one of my values to save, spend and give, but not all at once. An example is, I had pay raises over the years that gave me more income. I once had a situation where I had a payroll allotment of 300 per pay period to save for my kid's college tuition at the end of each semester and it helped me to not have to borrow money. So, when my kids were finished with college I took the 300 per pay period and added it to my 401k and put some back in my net pay, which helped me to save more money. After paying the tuition for so long I became accustomed to and built a habit of living without the money. As I progressed in my journey to better my situation I learned that having money in my account where I spend was not a good idea if I wanted to save more money. So, what I did back then and still works for me is, I have an account to pay bills with and a connected savings account to transfer money back and forth.

In addition, I keep a separate savings account at another bank with no ATM card so it's less easy access and cuts down on impulsive withdraws. This is my safeguard system against myself because I am human and not perfect. I am susceptible to the temptations that most of us have, I just try to stay aware of them and protect myself from myself. I will be honest I still get an urge from time to time to get back on the Titanic and have a good time till the ship sinks. This is probably because I feel that this Titanic sinking is what was once familiar to me years ago.

401K saving is a good thing and it can be especially good if we accept that its better than saving in a regular account, as far as a place to get a good return on our money. Bank savings accounts today don't pay any interest on your money like they used to, but they could when the rates go up. So, it's good to have a practice of saving because you can be ready to take advantage of higher rates when it happens. When your employer offers a 3% or 5% matching funds on your money, this can be looked at as 100% profit. If you put the maximum in like if 5% of your pay is $250, the company puts in your 401K $250, so you now have $500 deposited and on top of that you save some on your taxes. It really doesn't make sense not to take advantage of this if you have this opportunity.

Spot inventory: Doing a spot inventory helps us to reset our finances; it's only a quick on the spot budget, which helps us get a snapshot of how things look and whether there is any reason to start doing something or stop spending on something. We do this spot inventory with a simple budget using the example I provided or customize your own. This spot inventory can be employed even when you feel or sense you're getting off track.

Goals: Goals are important to set and accomplish, they can contribute to a healthy self-esteem. When we strive to accomplish our short and long-term goals, our esteem is affected. Your esteem is important because it has an impact on your life and choices. Self-esteem is important because, your esteem has a profound effect on your thinking, emotions, happiness, desires, values, and goals.

As Nathaniel Branden wrote about the importance of self-esteem, "Positive self- esteem is important because when people experience it, they feel and look good, are effective and productive, and they respond to others and themselves in healthy, positive, growing ways".

Self-esteem as it relates to personal finance, we set money goals small or large and try to accomplish them saving a little or a lot and we feel good about ourselves in the process. Like if we set a goal to earn a certain amount of money in a year or pay off a small amount on a credit card, each time we set a goal and accomplish it we keep the flame going and helping us to have a good spirit to set and achieve something else which may be greater. A lot of things can be esteem-able, work, school or service, however; we want to attach value to it and ourselves which makes us honestly feel good about ourselves is the point.

Financial Blessings: One of my biggest indirect financial and spiritual blessings has been my return on investing in my kids and others. I tried to pass on what teachings I got from my mother to my kids and some things I created, like helping them to build credit. When they were in their late teens I got them a credit card on my Visa by just adding them to my account. I then had them go to a few retailers that would give you instant credit if you presented a major credit card and they were able to establish their own credit and learn to be responsible. Many things have paid off with respect to my kids and others, I am very proud of my kids today with them being hard working responsible kids, now adults on their own and taking good care of themselves. I am grateful, this is a spiritual blessing as well. The word blessings also mean benefits and it can be said, what are benefits of saving, budgeting and having spiritual principles in your life? We have talked about benefits of saving and budgeting, but what about the benefit of budgeting your spirituality at the core. Between getting incoming spirituality and the unspiritual expense life has to offer. Giving to self and others with kindness, care and love add to the incoming side. Too much on your plate on the spending side can cause you to tilt, which can burden your efforts to grow and show up for life. Expenses like not taking care of your personal responsibilities of paying bills, not cutting back on expenses when needed and buying unneeded items, all contribute to weighing on our spirit affecting the core as well as our bank account. There never seems to be enough of the incoming spirit that will tilt the scale just more blessings to the core. There is a cost to even the rich for not taking care of their personal responsibilities, which they create their own problems with. Too much of anything can clutter your spirit. If we're not budgeting our finances very well, and not budgeting or managing our life and spirituality well, then we may want to take a deeper look at the link to what is in our core.

Winning Messages: Encourage yourself at your core being. Tell your core that your bad spending makes you sore, and you don't want it any more. You don't have to feel poor like you felt before. Get a new attitude and don't be rude. Fix yourself, wealth and financial health.

- Wealth by dishonesty will be diminished, but he who gathers by labor will increase. -Proverbs 12:25
- The blessing of the Lord makes one rich, and he adds no sorrow to it. -Proverbs 10:22
- Take an inventory of yourself. Are you too eager for passions? And he said to them. Take heed and beware of covetousness, for one's life does not consist of the things he possesses. – Luke: 12:15
- Putting your spending on paper daily or monthly makes it easy to see and harder to deny your true spending habits.

- Develop some patience with yourself, haste makes waste. Take your time with money, be slow to spend and quick to save.
- You reap what you sow, so if you sow a good seed into yourself chances are you will reap a good harvest in due season, even if it's to have a better acceptance of self.
- Money can answer all things, but it doesn't answer well to the spirit. Money is the lowest form of power for the spirit. It's good to have things as long as the things don't have you BROKE
- Giving is a blessing, in giving you may receive spiritually. Keep some humility about your giving, because without the right attitude about giving we may brag about our giving and give our blessing away.
- Being in the dark about your finances can create a monster. But budgeting can kill these self- created monsters with the light of exposure from the pen to the paper.
- It's possible that if you put money before your god you may lose it. But seek first the kingdom of God and his rightness and all these things shall be added to you. Matthew 6:33
- The love of money is the root of all its evil. Ecclesiastes 5:10. Money should be valued as a thing and not a power unconquerable.
- A budgeting practice helps to establish a new healthy habit and a budget conscious.
- There are two types of people, givers, and takers. Givers always seem to have, and takers always are in need.
- Just like you would caution yourself by reading the nutrition label when you're being health conscious before you buy and eat something. In the same way, you can caution yourself with spending your money by reading your account balance and the last budget entry before you spend.

- You don't have to worry if you're heading towards financial glory, because that's how we want to end our story. I heard it said that it's not as important how you start but how you finish that's more important. I want to say hallelujah, don't let the good times fool you because you still must stay in the light that schooled You!
- A wise man learns from his mistakes and a wiser man learns from the mistakes of others.

Help is available to us all, but we must reach out for it.

Here is a helping hand below.

Credit counseling: for a list of approved credit counseling agencies by state.

Go to https://www.justice.gov/ust/list-credit-counseling-agencies-approved-pursuant-11-usc-111

Small business administration: good to partnership with when you're starting a business. www.sbc.gov 800-827-5722

Score business association: which is backed by the SBC and has great resources for when you're new to starting your own business. They also have mentors at Score. The address is www.score.org 800-6340245 current business address is 1175 Herndon Parkway, Suite 900. Herndon, VA. 20170

Free budget calculator by Quicken.
https://www.quicken.com/budget-calculator

United Way: is a great resource for those on their way back up or those looking up to get better. www.unitedway.org also they have a title on the web site called My smart money which includes a tool called calculate my financial health. 211 help line, Also free online tax software by HR block.
https://www.unitedway.org/myfreetaxes/resources/hr-block

INCOME		EXPENSES	
CASH	_____	Mtg/Rent	_____
		ELECTRIC	_____
SALARIES	_____	GAS	_____
		PHONES	_____
		CABLE	_____
		INTERNET	_____
		MEDICAL	_____
		CAR INS	_____
		LIFE INS	_____
		2ND MTG	_____
		CAR LOAN	_____
		CHILDCARE	_____
		CAR GAS	_____
		VISA	_____
		MASTER	_____
		CREDIT	_____
		PET CARE	_____
		ALLOWANCE	_____
		SAVINGS	_____
		MISC.	_____
		MISC.	_____
		MISC.	_____

TOTAL INCOME _____ >CARRY FOWARD> > _____

TOTAL EXPENSES _____

BALANCE POSITIVE SAVED BALANCE NEGATIVE CUT BACK EXP. _____ > C/F

ALL RIGHTS RESERVED, WHICH

INCLUDES THE RIGHT TO REPRODUCE

THIS MANUAL/BOOK, IN ANY FORM

EXCEPT AS PROVIDED BY U.S. COPYRIGHT

COPYRIGHT 2017 BY JAMES F. LUCAS JR.

www.ingramcontent.com/pod-product-compliance
Lightning Source LLC
Chambersburg PA
CBHW030516220526
45464CB00006B/2819